Have Yourself a MERRY LITTLE CHRISTMAS and Other Holiday Favorites

ISBN 978-1-4803-5130-1

HAL•LEONARD® CORPORATION

7777 W. BLUEMOUND RD. P.O. BOX 13819 MILWAUKEE, WI 53213

Visit Hal Leonard Online at
www.halleonard.com

THE CHRISTMAS WALTZ

Words by SAMMY CAHN
Music by JULE STYNE

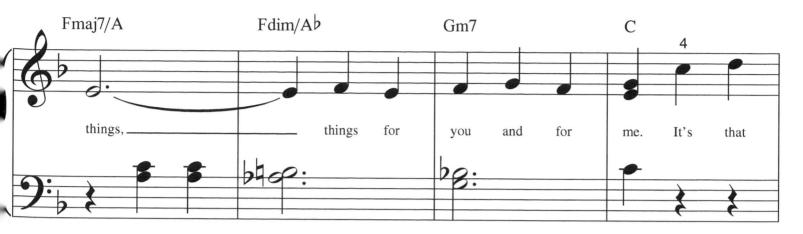

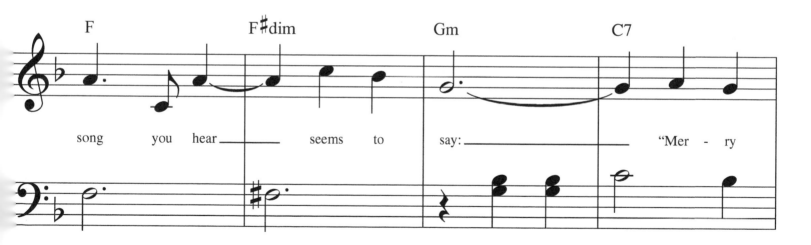

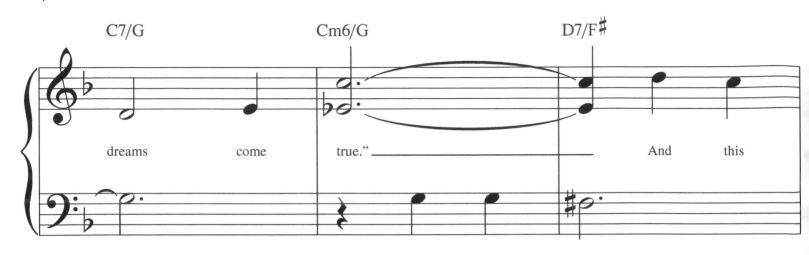

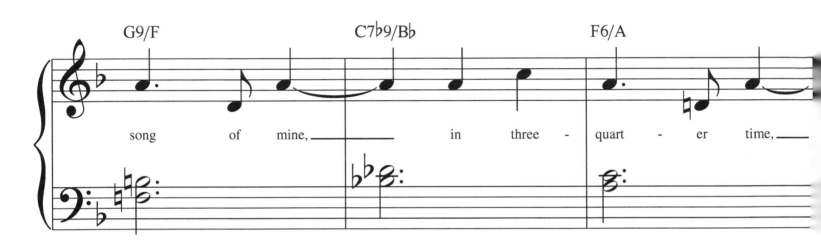

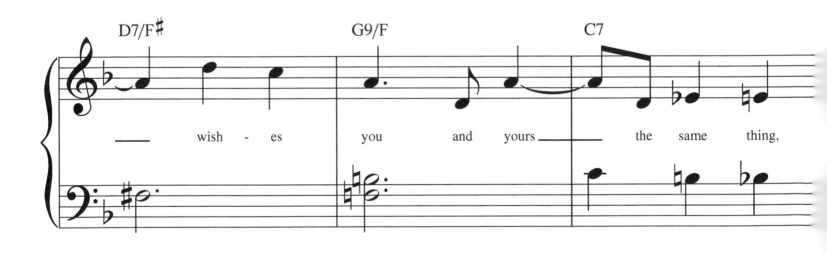

ALL I WANT FOR CHRISTMAS IS MY TWO FRONT TEETH

Words and Music by
DON GARDNER

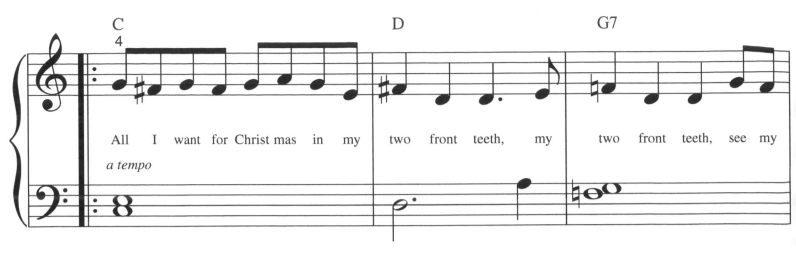

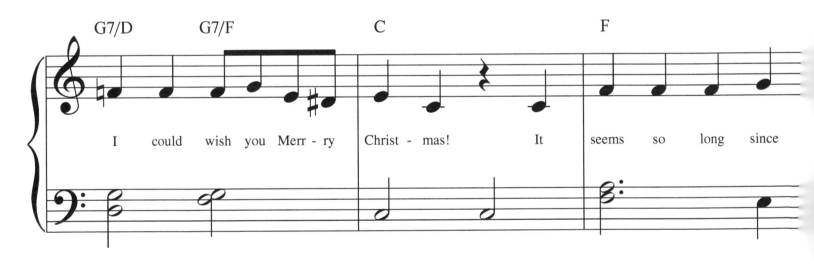

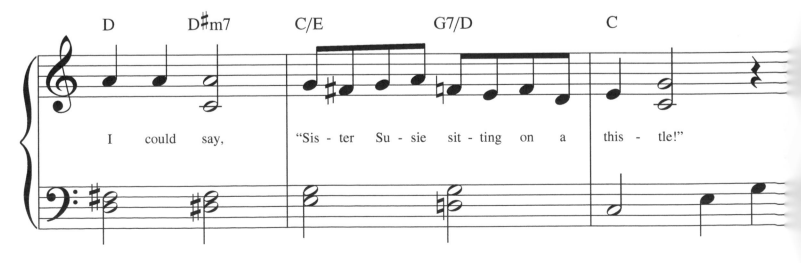

Gosh, oh gee, how hap - py I'd be, if I could on - ly whis - tle!

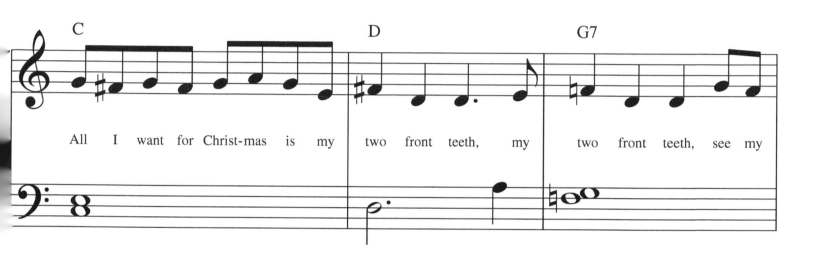

All I want for Christ-mas is my two front teeth, my two front teeth, see my

two front teeth! Gee, if I could on - ly have my two front teeth, then

rit.

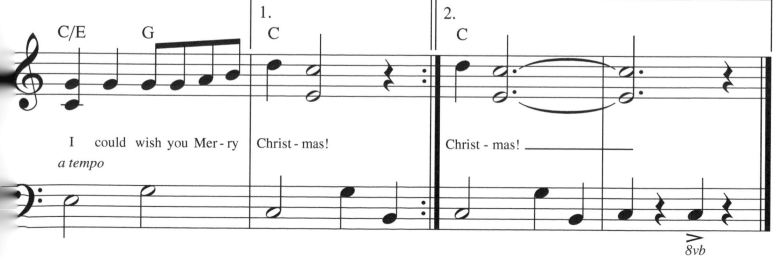

I could wish you Mer - ry Christ - mas! Christ - mas!

a tempo

8vb

C-H-R-I-S-T-M-A-S

Words by JENNY LOU CARSON
Music by EDDY ARNOLD

diff - 'rent   when   moth - er   sat   me   down   and

taught   me   to   spell   Christ - mas   this   way. _____

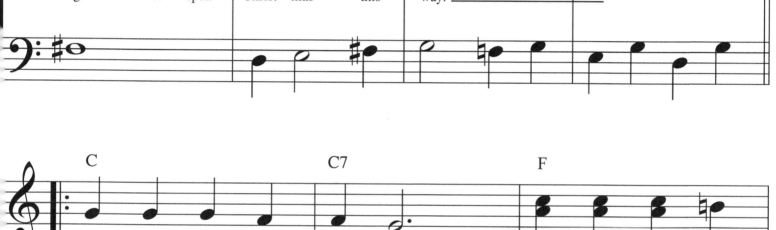

"C"   is   for   the   Christ   child.   born   up - on   this

day.   "H"   for   her - ald   an - gels   in   the

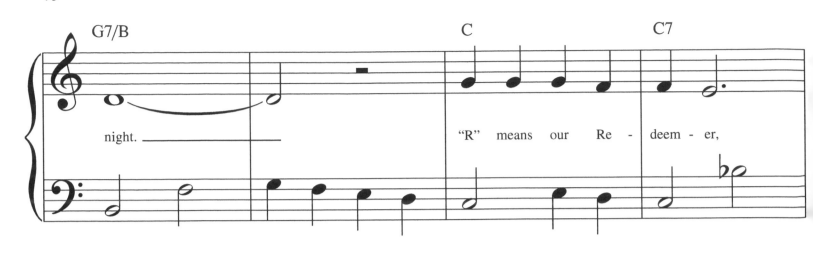

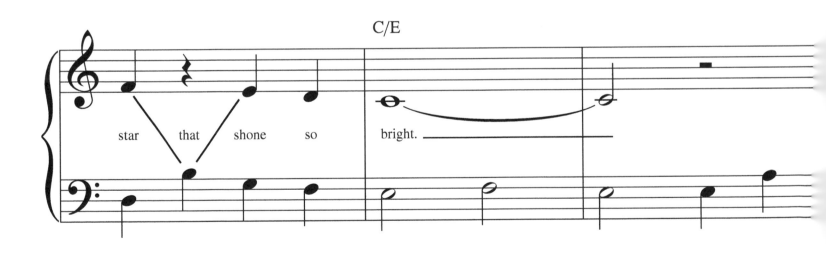

CHRISTMAS AULD LANG SYNE

Words and Music by MANN CURTIS
and FRANK MILITARY

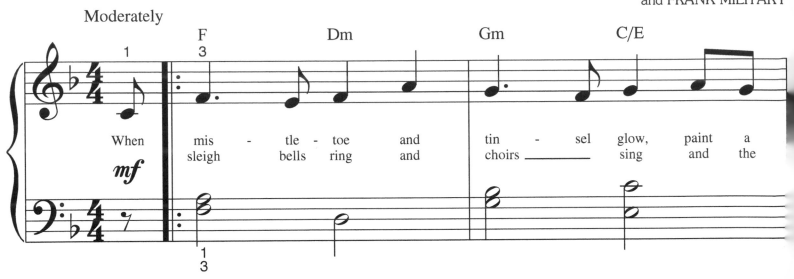

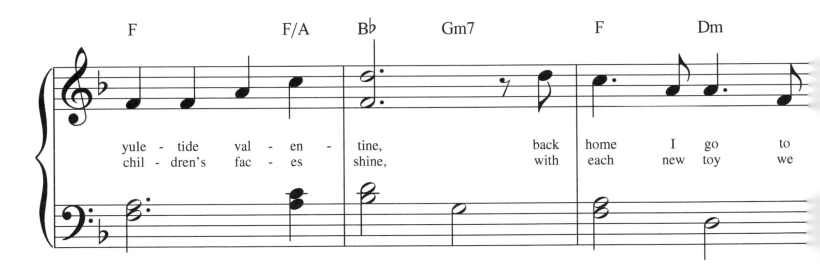

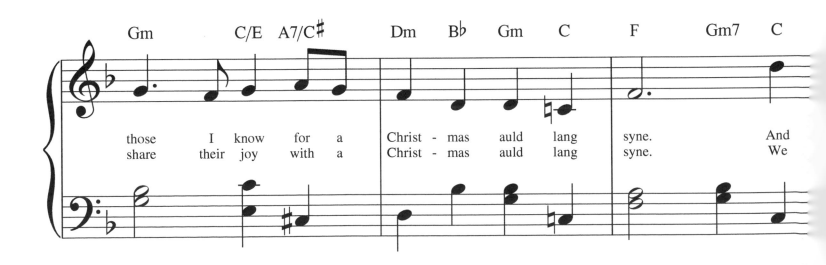

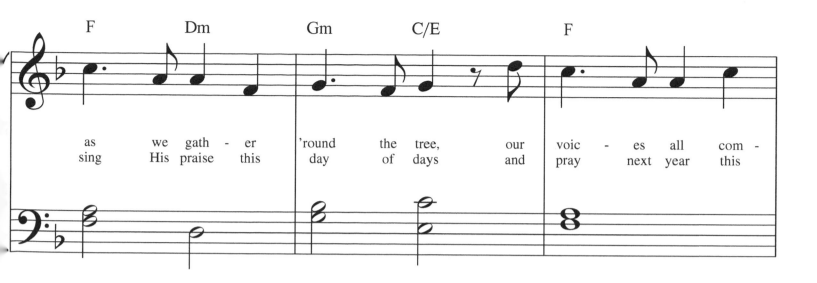

as we gath - er 'round the tree, our voic - es all com -
sing His praise this day of days and pray next year this

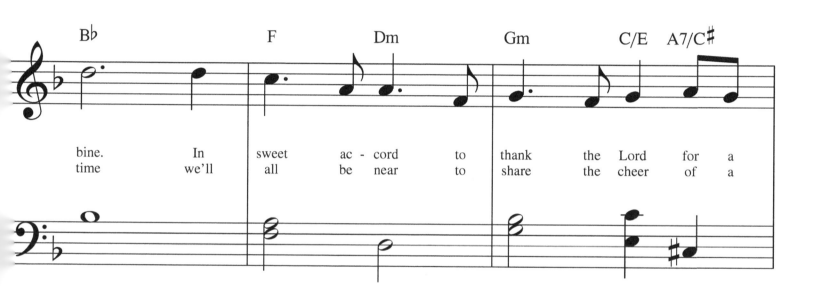

bine. In sweet ac - cord to thank the Lord for a
time we'll all be near to share the cheer of a

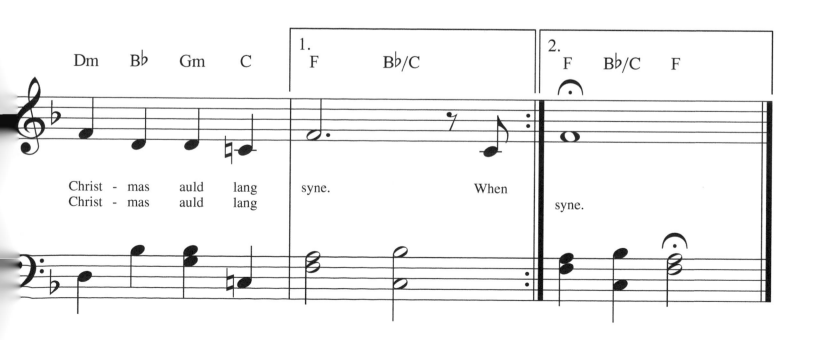

Christ - mas auld lang syne. When
Christ - mas auld lang syne.

CHRISTMAS IN KILLARNEY

Words and Music by JOHN REDMOND
and FRANK WELDON

GOIN' ON A SLEIGHRIDE

Words and Music by
RALPH BLANE

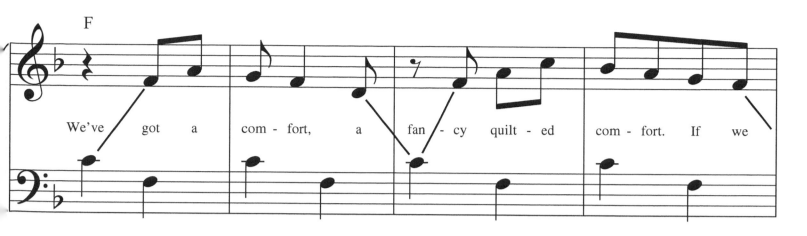

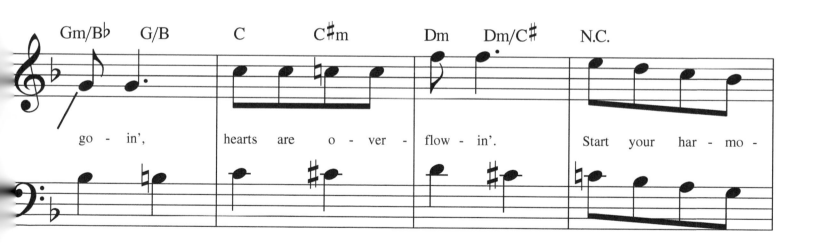

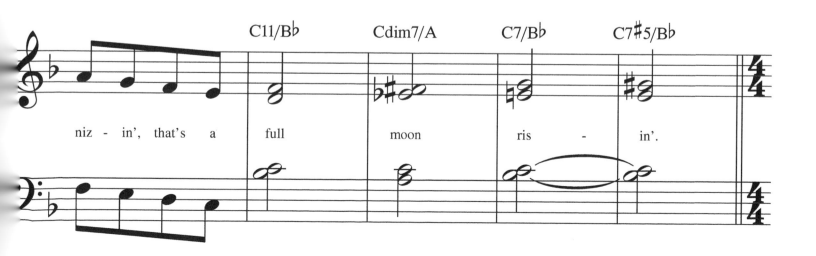

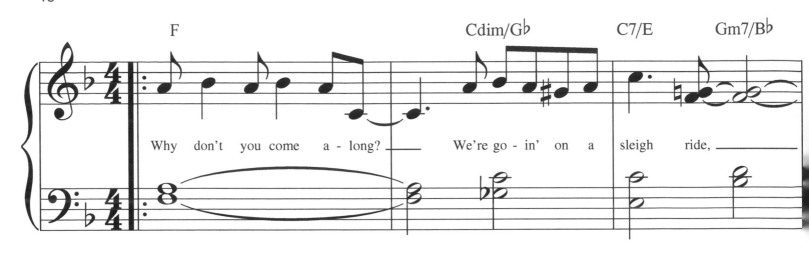

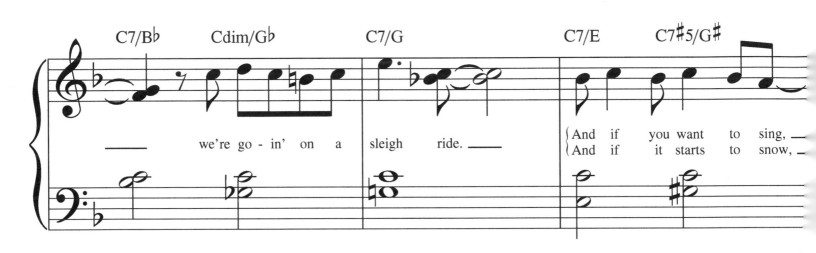

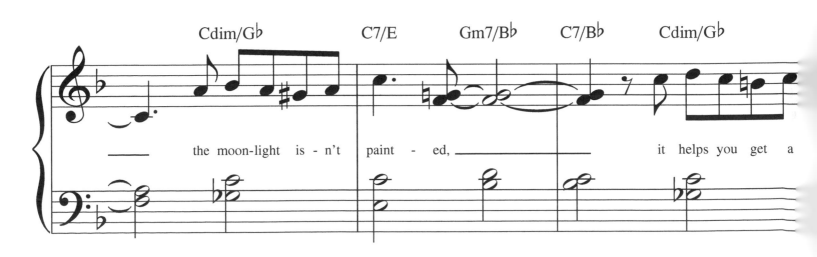

trust in that moon a - bove, _____ and when the sleigh- ride's o - ver, _____

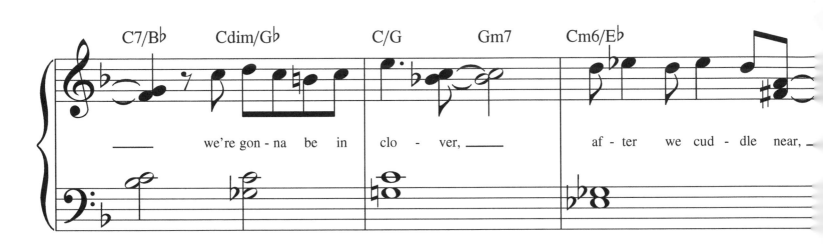

_____ we're gon - na be in clo - ver, _____ af - ter we cud - dle near, _____

_____ may - be we'll find that we're in

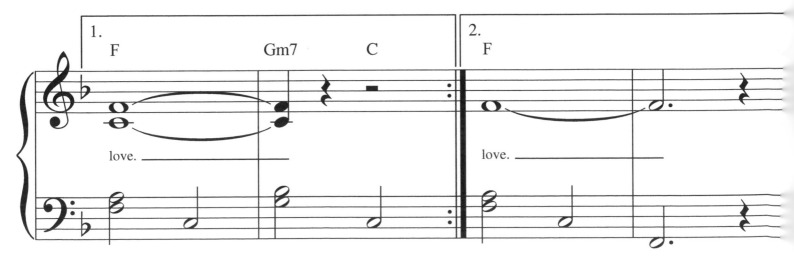

1. love. _____

2. love. _____

GROWN-UP CHRISTMAS LIST

Words and Music by DAVID FOSTER
and LINDA THOMPSON-JENNER

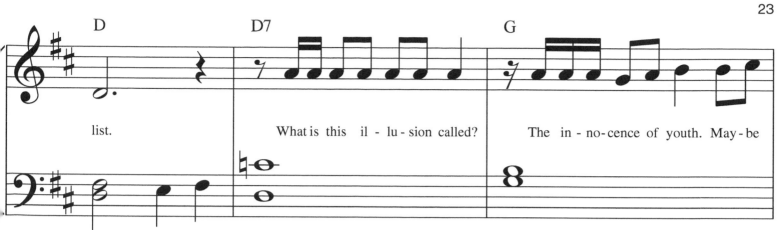

list. What is this il - lu - sion called? The in - no - cence of youth. May - be

D.S. al Coda

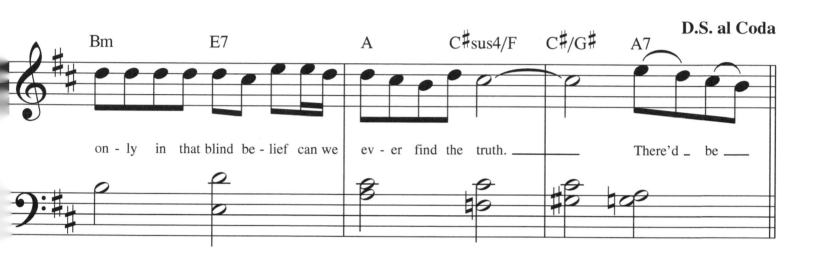

on - ly in that blind be - lief can we ev - er find the truth. ____ There'd _ be ____

CODA

list. This is my on - ly life - long wish. _ This is my grown - up

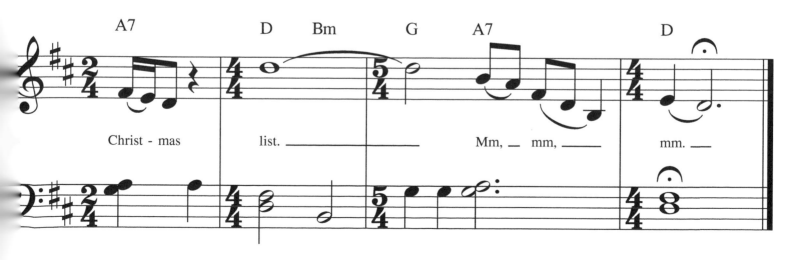

Christ - mas list. ____ Mm, _ mm, ____ mm. ____

THE GREATEST GIFT OF ALL

Words and Music
JOHN JARV

Moderately, with feeling

Dawn is slow - ly

break - ing,   our friends have   all   gone

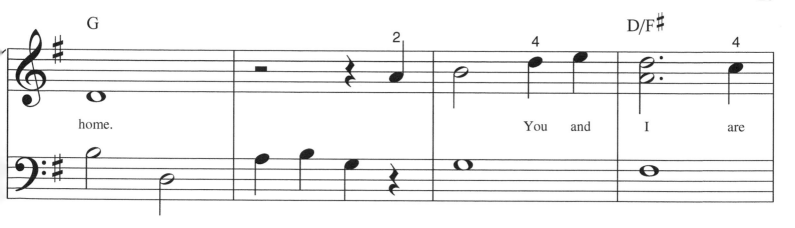

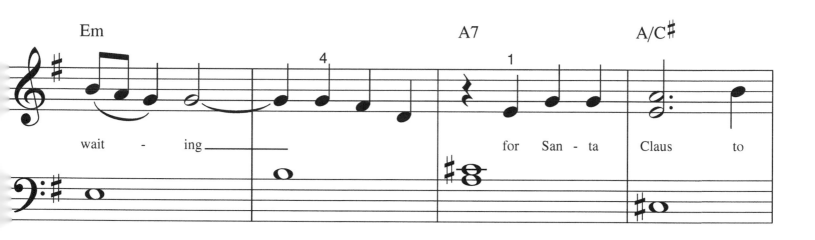

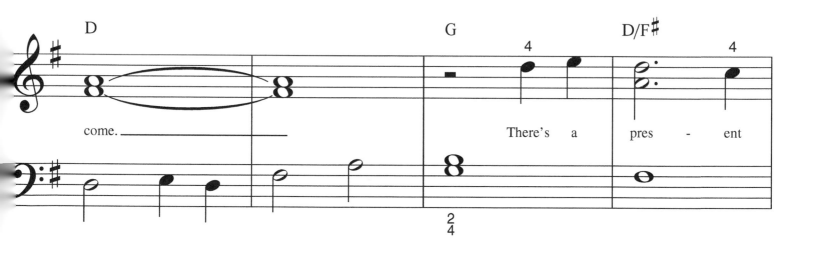

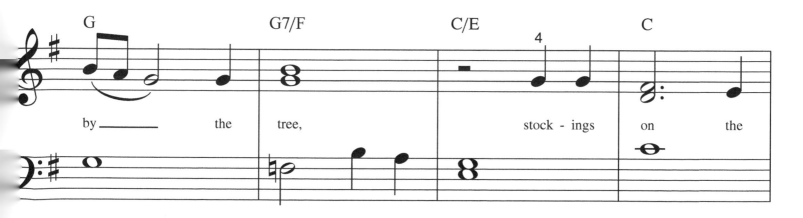

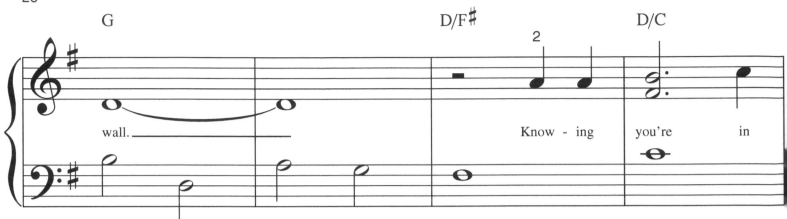

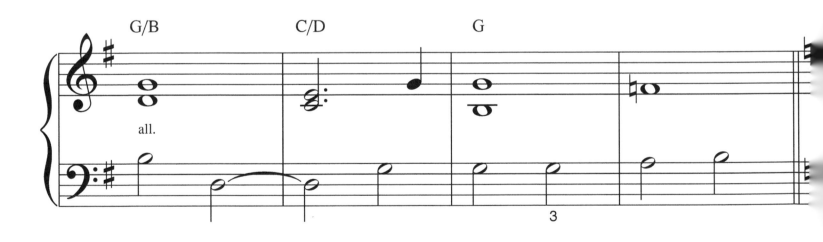

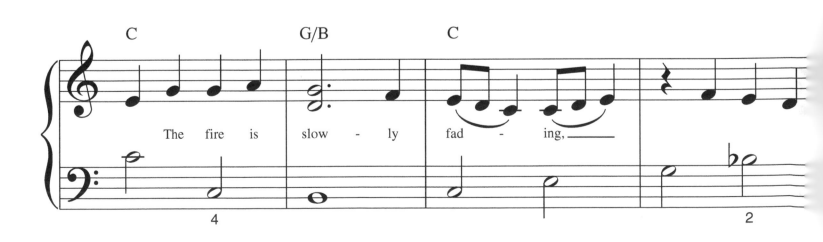

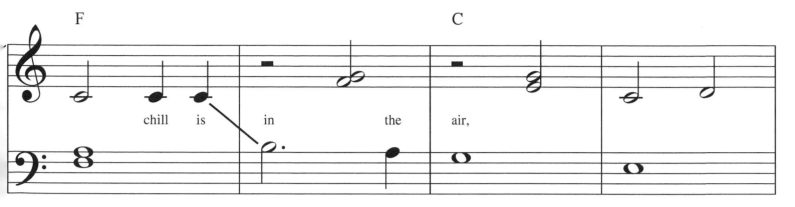

chill is in the air,

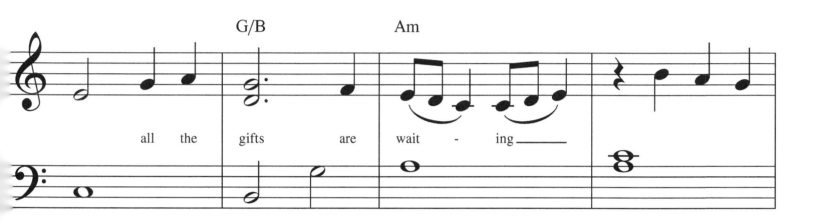

all the gifts are wait - ing____

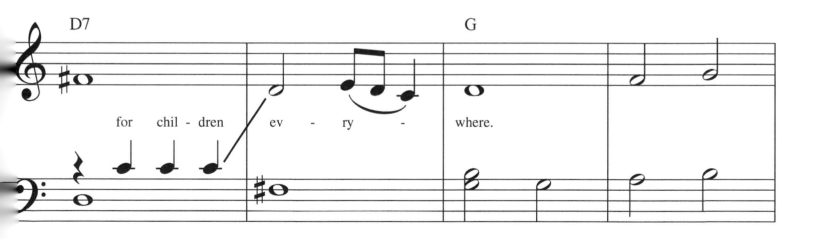

for chil - dren ev - ry - where.

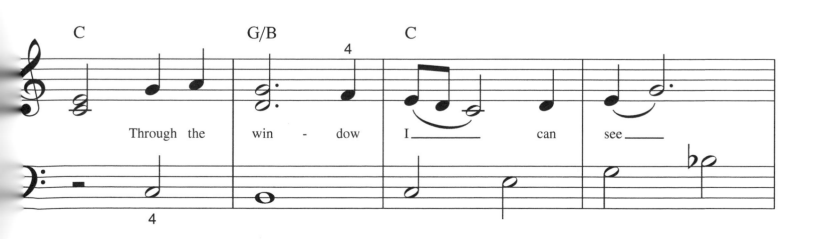

Through the win - dow I____ can see____

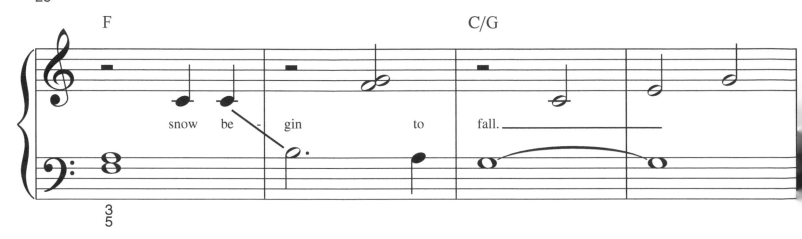

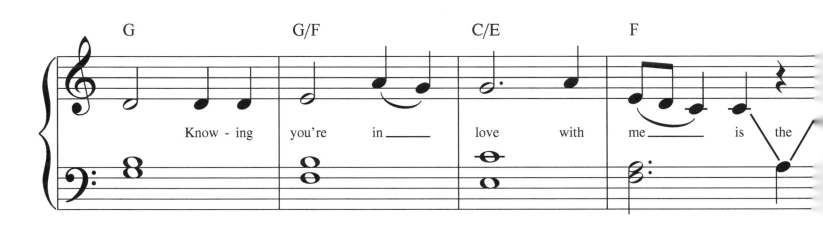

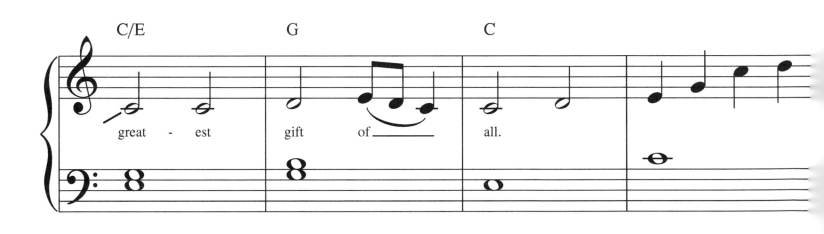

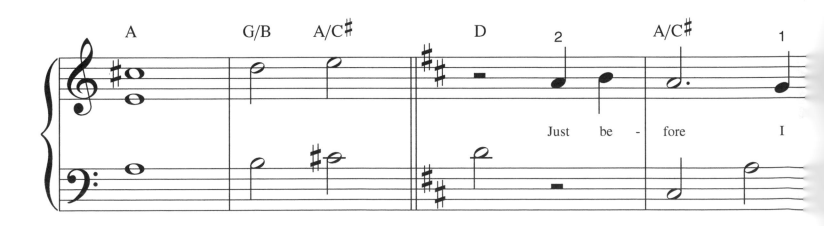

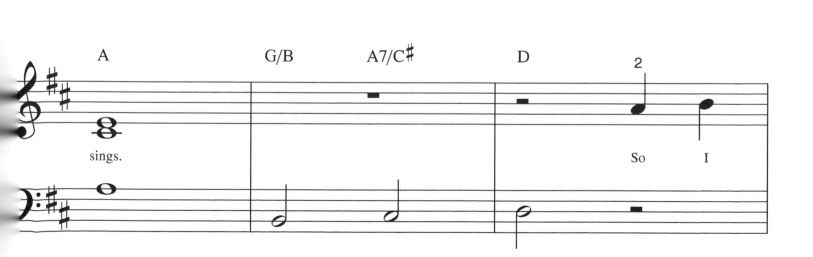

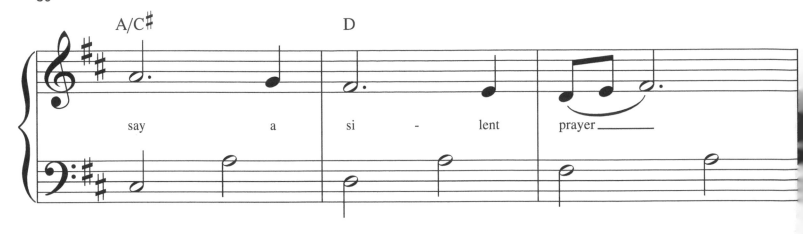

say a si - lent prayer

for crea - tures great and small.

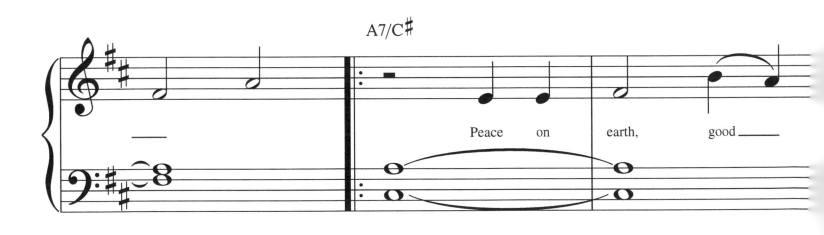

Peace on earth, good

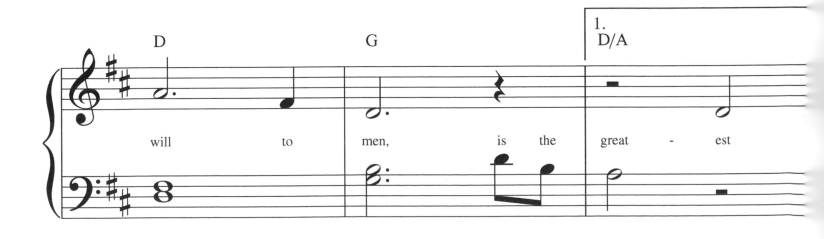

will to men, is the great - est

HAVE YOURSELF A MERRY LITTLE CHRISTMAS

from MEET ME IN ST. LOUIS

Words and Music by HUGH MARTIN
and RALPH BLANE

Slowly

Have your-self a mer-ry lit-tle Christ-mas, let your heart be
Have your-self a mer-ry lit-tle Christ-mas, make the Yule-tide

mf

With pedal

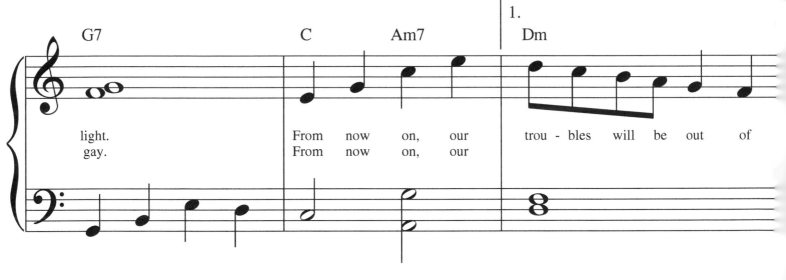

light.   From now on, our   trou-bles will be out of
gay.   From now on, our

1.

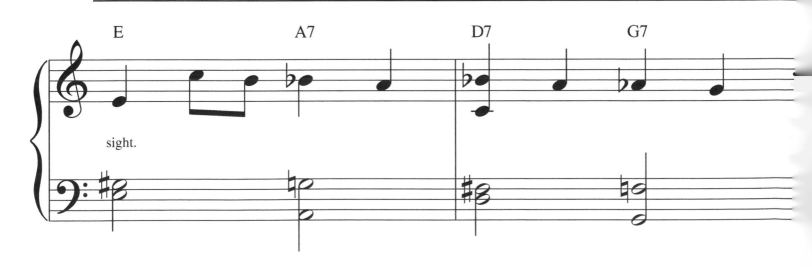

sight.

HERE COMES SANTA CLAUS
(Right Down Santa Claus Lane)

Words and Music by GENE AUTRY
and OAKLEY HALDEMAN

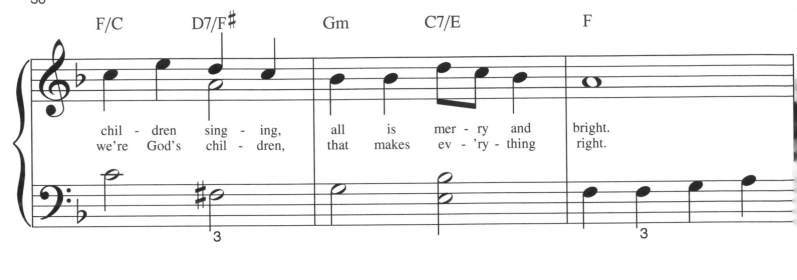

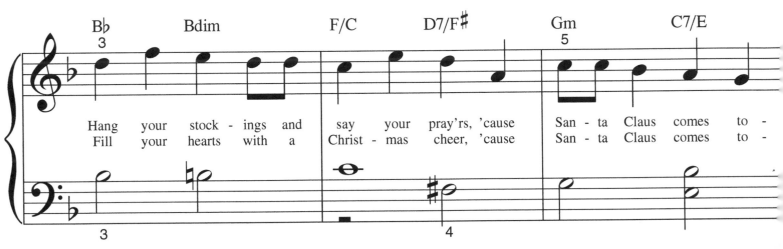

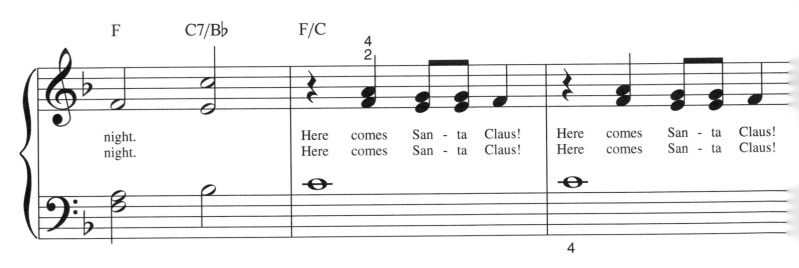

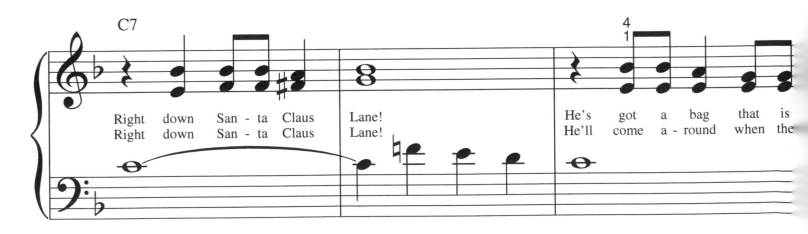

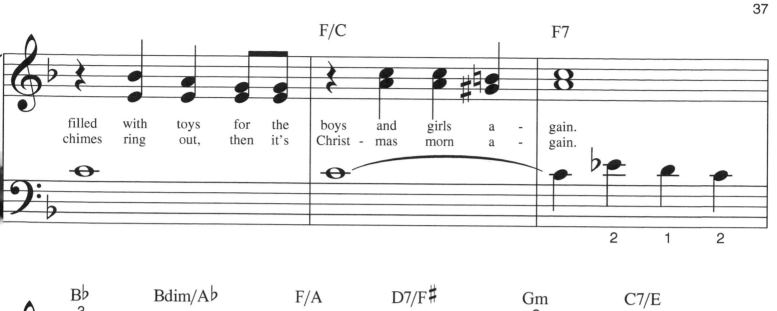

filled with toys for the boys and girls a - gain.
chimes ring out, then it's Christ - mas morn a - gain.

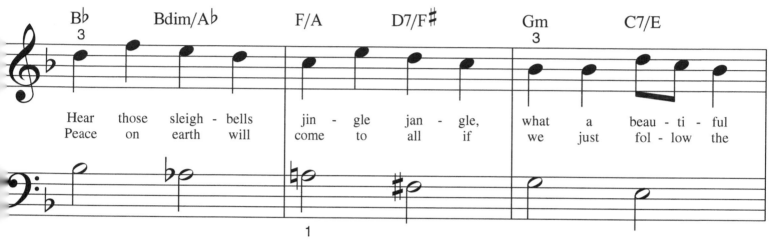

Hear those sleigh - bells jin - gle jan - gle, what a beau - ti - ful
Peace on earth will come to all if we just fol - low the

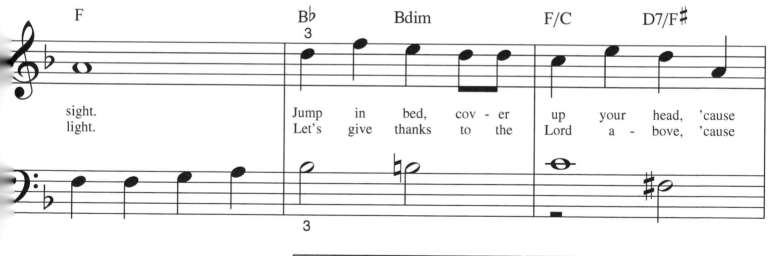

sight.
light.

Jump in bed, cov - er up your head, 'cause
Let's give thanks to the Lord a - bove, 'cause

San - ta Claus comes to - night.
San - ta Claus comes to - night.

MISTLETOE AND HOLLY

Words and Music by FRANK SINATRA,
DOK STANFORD and HENRY W. SANICOLA

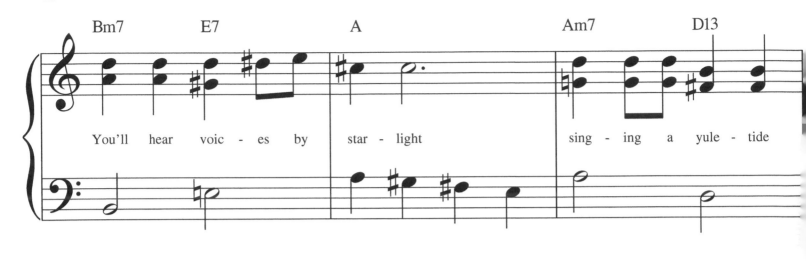

You'll hear voic - es by star - light sing - ing a yule - tide

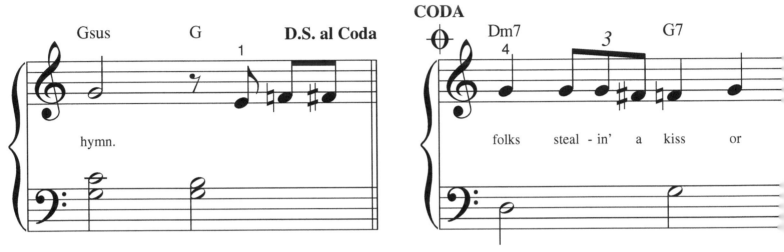

hymn.

D.S. al Coda

CODA

folks steal - in' a kiss or

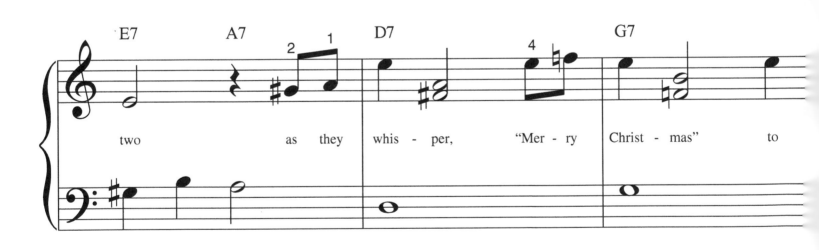

two as they whis - per, "Mer - ry Christ - mas" to

you.

LET'S MAKE IT CHRISTMAS ALL YEAR 'ROUND

Words by DOROTHY FIELDS
Music by BURTON LANE

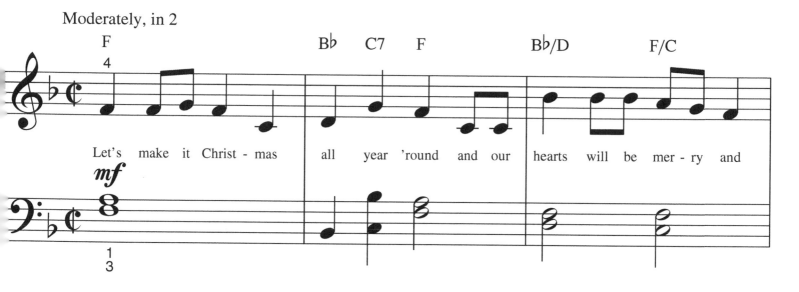

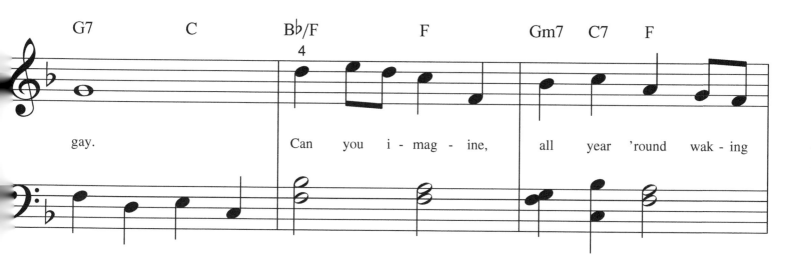

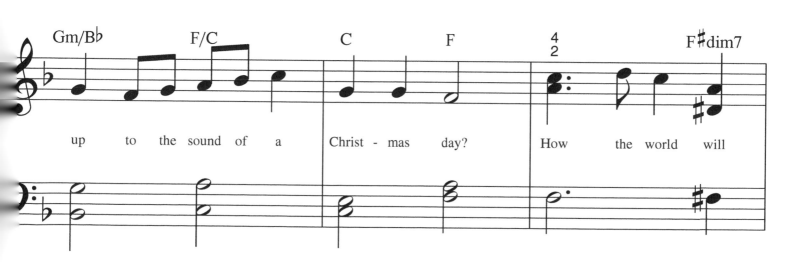

dance and sing of peace on earth at last. A

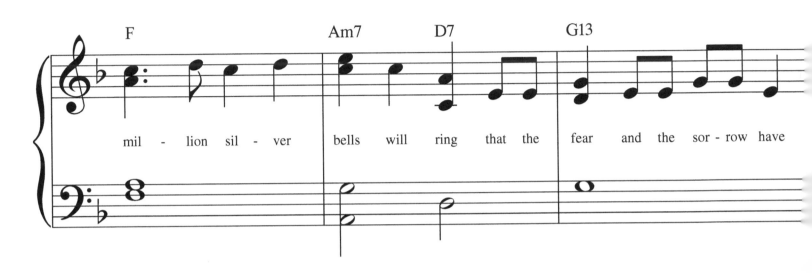

mil - lion sil - ver bells will ring that the fear and the sor - row have

passed. Oh, why is it on - ly on this day that the

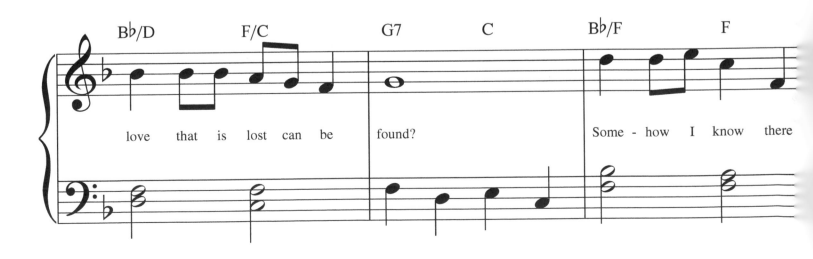

love that is lost can be found? Some - how I know there

THE LITTLE DRUMMER BOY

Words and Music by HARRY SIMEONE,
HENRY ONORATI and KATHERINE DAVIS

F
2
3
to lay be - fore the King, pa -
that's fit to give our King, pa -
F7
B♭
5
F
5
C
rum pum pum pum, rum pum pum pum, rum pum pum pum,
rum pum pum pum, rum pum pum pum, rum pum pum pum.
F
1
so to hon - or Him, pa -
Shall I play for you, pa -
1.
C
F
(D.C.)
rum pum pum pum, when we come.
rum pum pum pum, on my drum?

NUTTIN' FOR CHRISTMAS

Words and Music by SID TEPPER
and ROY C. BENNETT

SANTA CLAUS IS COMIN' TO TOWN

Words by HAVEN GILLESPIE
Music by J. FRED COOTS

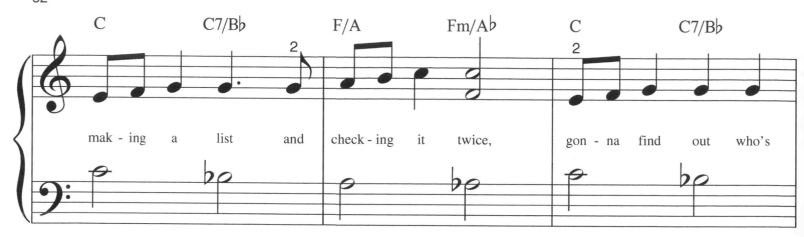

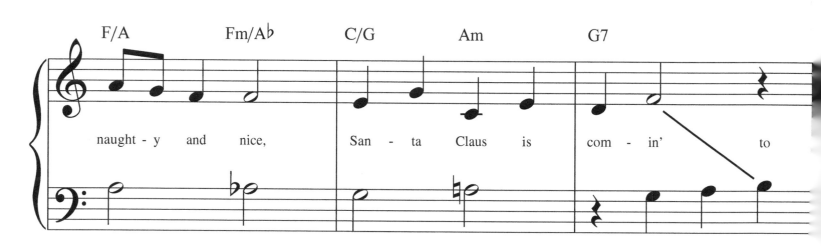

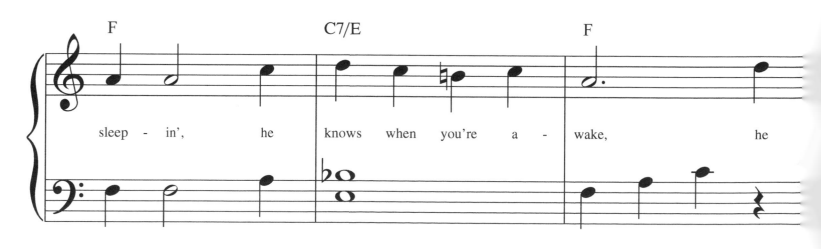

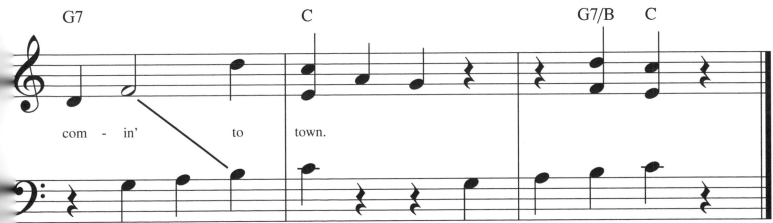

SLEIGH RIDE

Music by LEROY ANDERSON
Words by MITCHELL PARISH

SNOWFALL

Lyrics by RUTH THORNHILL
Music by CLAUDE THORNHILL

Snow - flakes _____ whis - per _____

_____ 'neath my _____

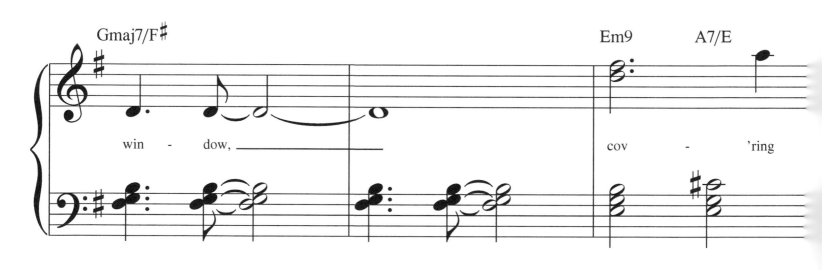

win - dow, _____ cov - 'ring

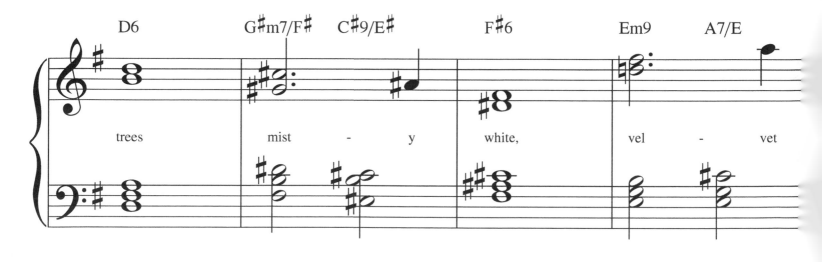

trees mist - y white, vel - vet

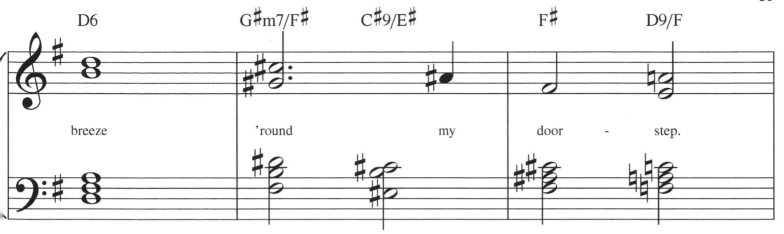

breeze   'round   my   door - step.

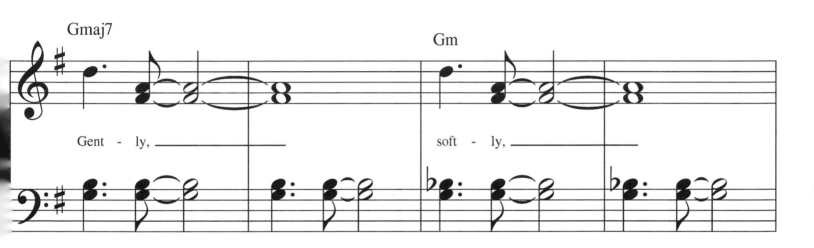

Gent - ly, _____   soft - ly, _____

si - lent _____   snow - fall. _____

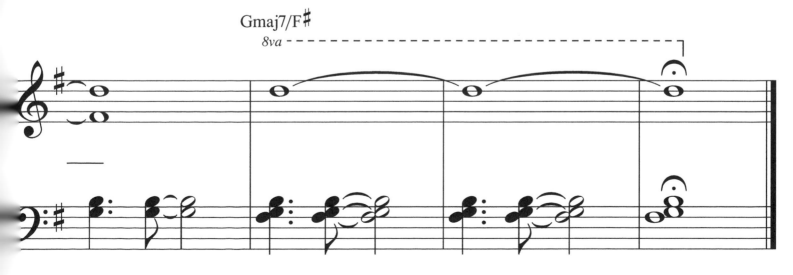

SOMEWHERE IN MY MEMORY
from the Twentieth Century Fox Motion Picture HOME ALONE

Words by LESLIE BRICUSSE
Music by JOHN WILLIAMS

all of the mu - sic,   all of the mag - ic,

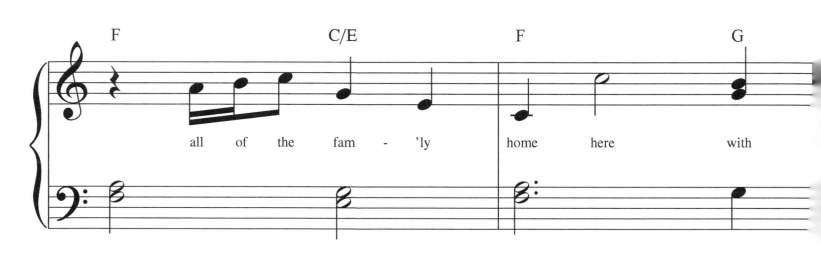

all of the fam - 'ly   home here   with

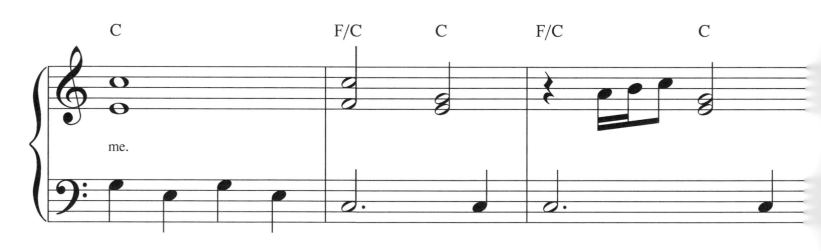

me.

SUZY SNOWFLAKE

Words and Music by SID TEPPER
and ROY BENNETT

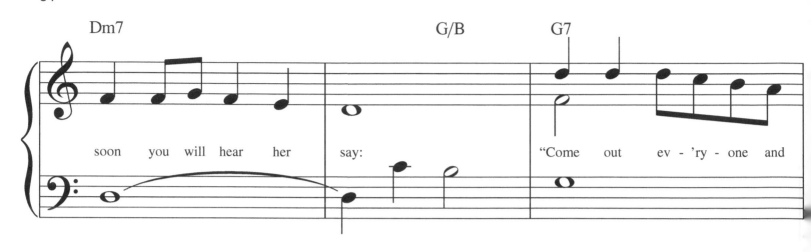

Dm7 · G/B · G7

soon you will hear her say: "Come out ev-'ry-one and

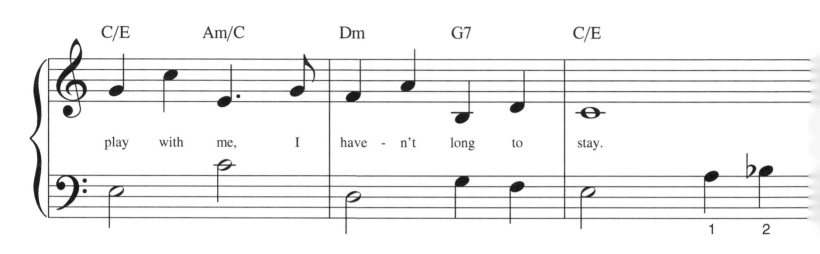

C/E · Am/C · Dm · G7 · C/E

play with me, I have-n't long to stay.

1   2

F · C/E · G/D

If you wan-na make a snow-man I'll help you make one,

1   2

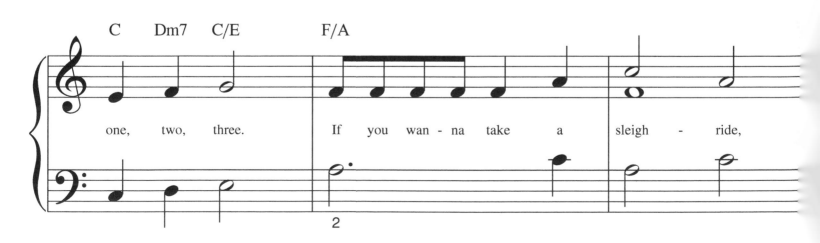

C · Dm7 · C/E · F/A

one, two, three. If you wan-na take a sleigh-ride,

2

TENNESSEE CHRISTMAS

Words and Music by AMY GRANT
and GARY CHAPMAN

Den - ver snow fall - in'. Some - bod - y said it's four feet ___ deep. But
we'd have it made there. Bring home a tan for New Year's _ Eve.

it does - n't mat - ter, give me the laugh - ter, I'm gon - na choose to ___
Sure sounds ex - cit - ing, aw - fully in - vit - ing, still I think I'm gon - na

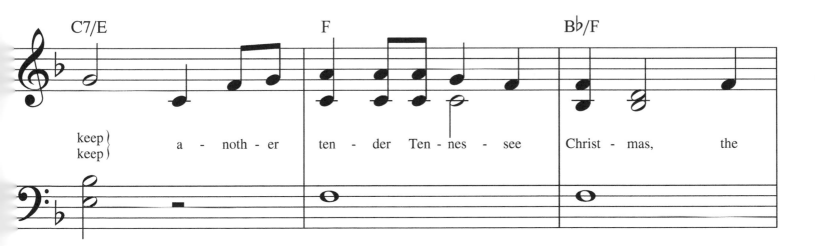

keep }
keep } a - noth - er ten - der Ten - nes - see Christ - mas, the

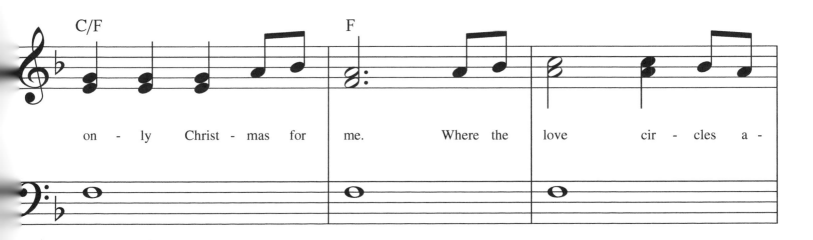

on - ly Christ - mas for me. Where the love cir - cles a -

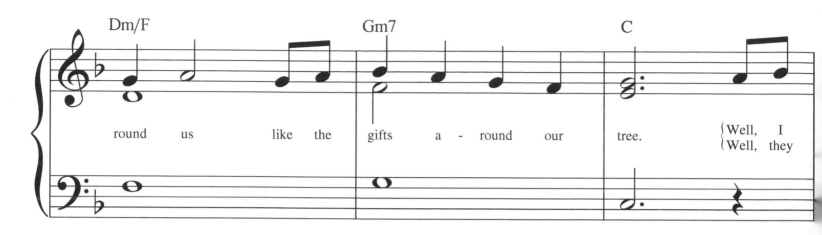

round us like the   gifts a - round our   tree.   { Well, I
{ Well, they

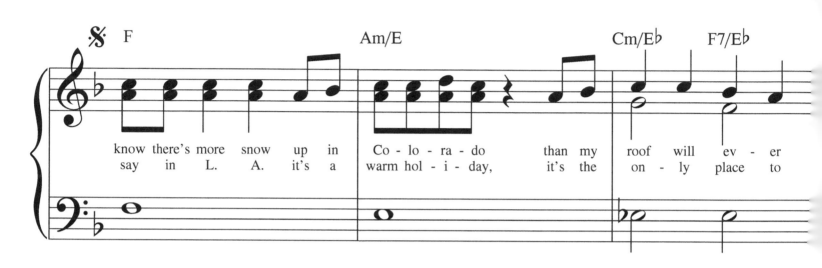

know there's more snow up in   Co - lo - ra - do   than my   roof will ev - er
say in L. A. it's a   warm hol - i - day,   it's the   on - ly place to

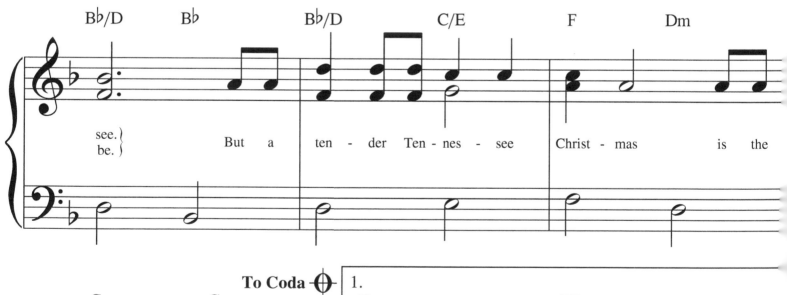

see. }   But a ten - der Ten - nes - see   Christ - mas   is the
be. }

To Coda

1.

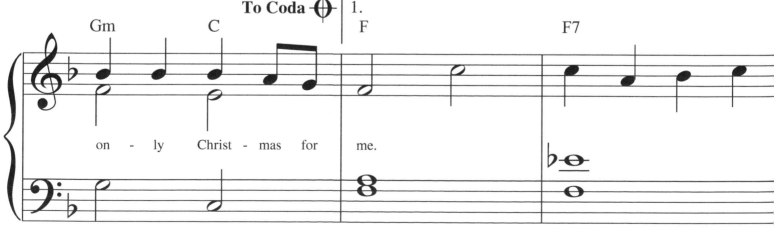

on - ly Christ - mas for   me.

THAT CHRISTMAS FEELING

Words and Music by BENNIE BENJAMIN
and GEORGE DAVID WEISS

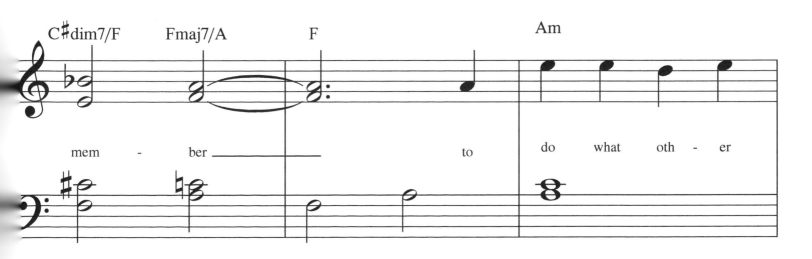

UP ON THE HOUSETOP

Words and Music by
B.R. HANBY

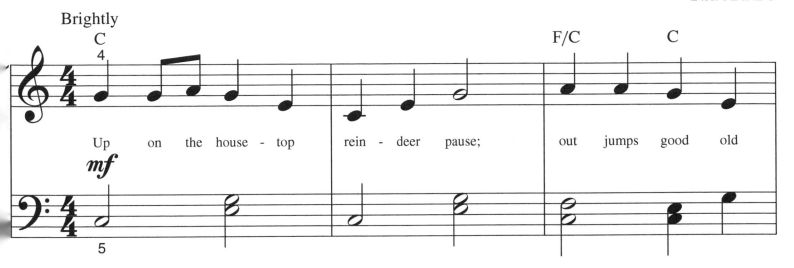

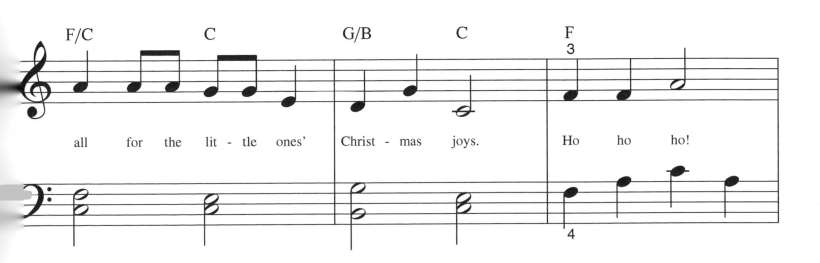

TOYLAND
from BABES IN TOYLAND

Words by GLEN MacDONOUGH
Music by VICTOR HERBERT

WHITE CHRISTMAS
from the Motion Picture Irving Berlin's HOLIDAY INN

Words and Music by
IRVING BERLIN

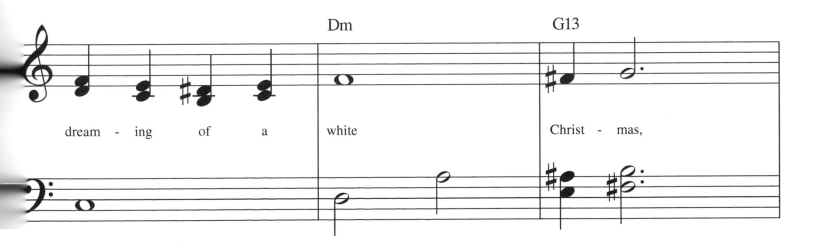

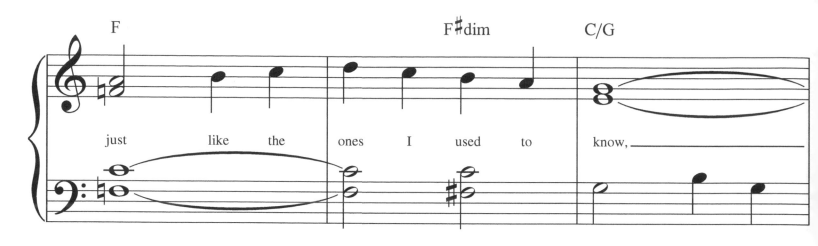

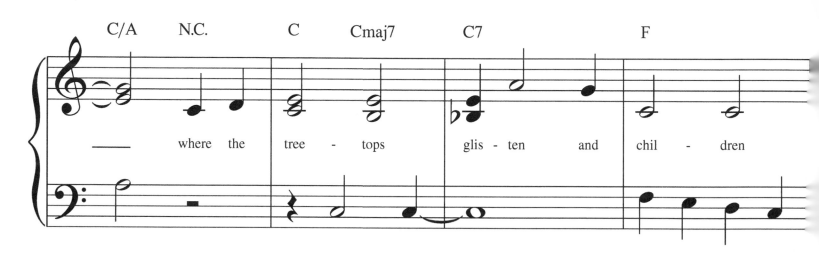

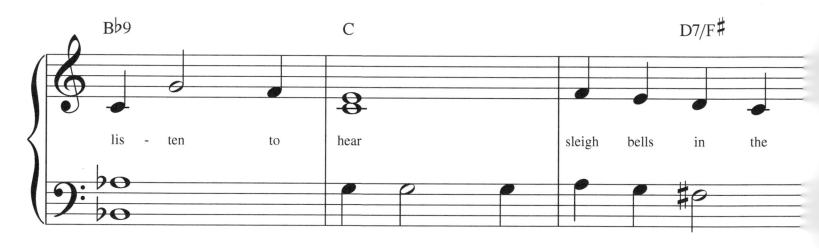

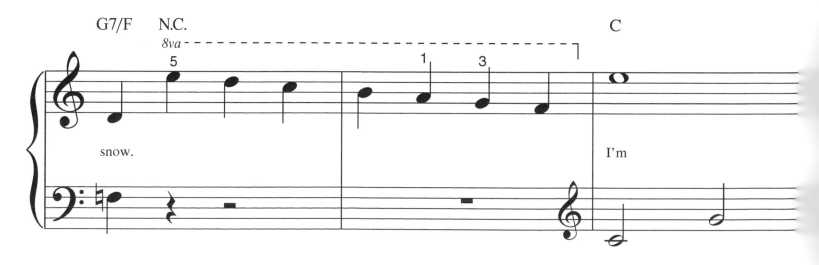

81

WINTER WONDERLAND

Words by DICK SMITH
Music by FELIX BERNARD

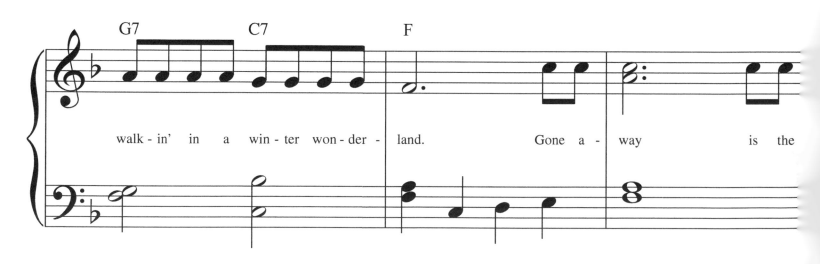

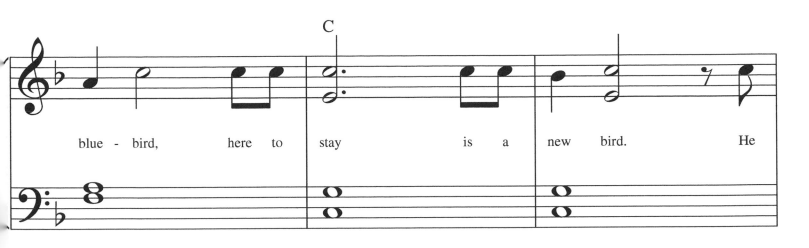

blue - bird, here to stay is a new bird. He

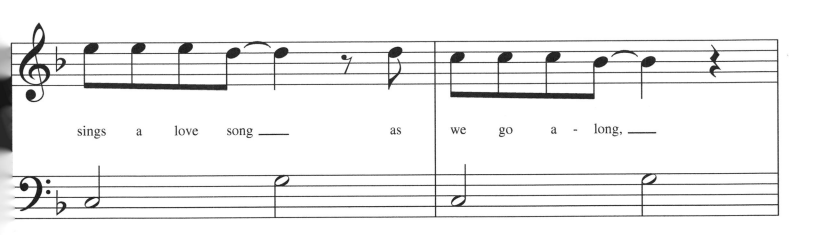

sings a love song _____ as we go a - long, _____

walk - in' in a win - ter won - der - land!

In the mead - ow we can build a snow - man,
In the mead - ow we can build a snow - man,

WHAT ARE YOU DOING NEW YEAR'S EVE?

By FRANK LOESSER

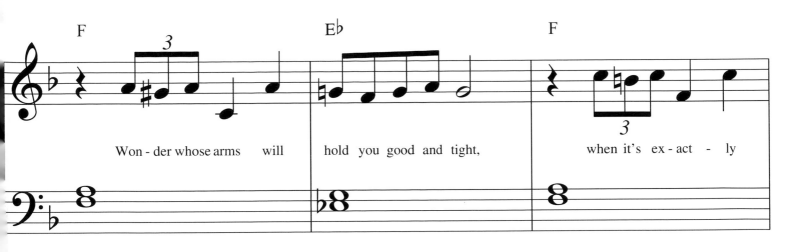

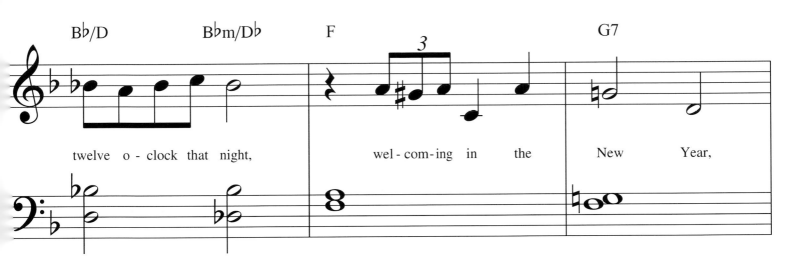

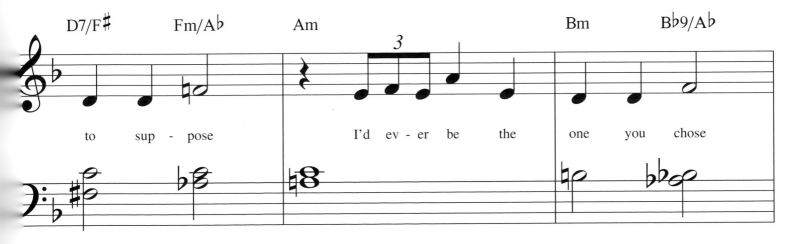

88

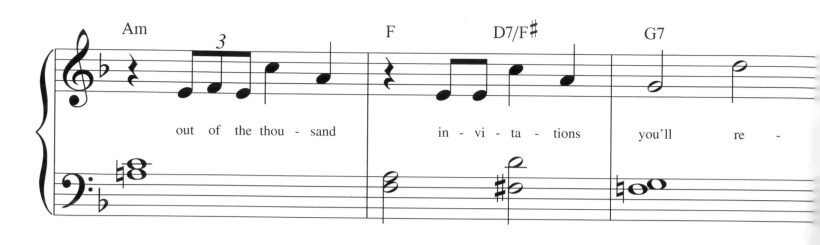

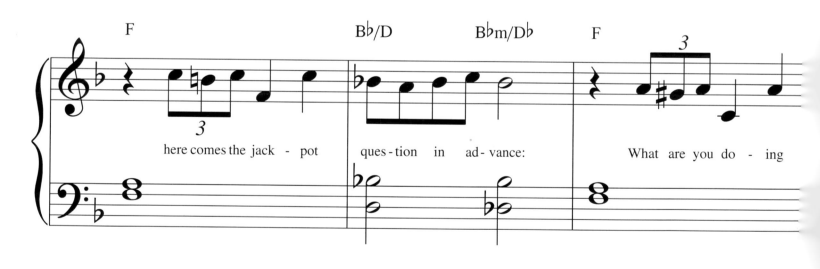

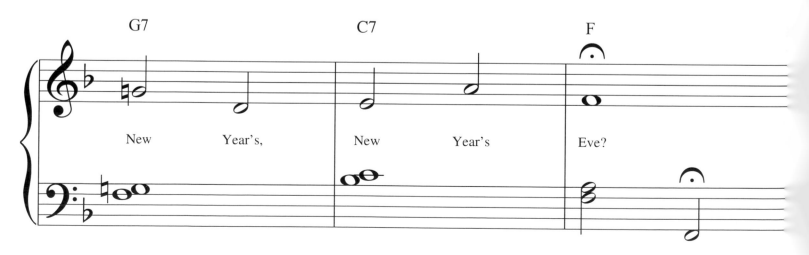